QUATTRO™

THE POCKET REFERENCE

Stephen Cobb

Osborne **McGraw-Hill**
Berkeley, California

Osborne **McGraw-Hill**
2600 Tenth Street
Berkeley, California 94710
U.S.A.

For information on translations and book distributors outside of the U.S.A., please write to Osborne **McGraw-Hill** at the above address.

Quattro™ : The Pocket Reference

1234567890 DODO 898

ISBN 0-07-881378-6

Copy Editor: Kay Luthin
Word Processor: Bonnie Bozorg
Proofreader: Barbara Conway
Production Supervisor: Kevin Shafer

CONTENTS

INTRODUCTION

This pocket guide is designed to serve as a reference for Quattro users, from the novice to the experienced. Quattro's features are presented in a way that makes it easy to find a description of any feature about which you want to read. If you are a new user of Quattro you will find it convenient to keep this guide beside you as you learn to use the program. If you are a more experienced user, you can look up features you have not yet used or remind yourself of features that you use infrequently.

The guide groups all of the commands in logical sections, and then presents the rules of formula and macro writing. At the end of this guide are a number of useful lists, including display formats and their codes, the @ functions, macros and macro commands, commonly used keys, and cursor-movement, file-list, and Edit mode keys.

ADVANCED COMMANDS

The /Advanced command group consists of five sophisticated commands used for database operations and numerical or statistical analysis. When you select the /Advanced command from the Quattro menu, you will see the following options: Database, What-if, Regression, Frequency, Matrix, and Quit. Since these five commands all have numerous options, they are dealt with in their own sections. The Quit option is used to remove the Advanced menu, which will remain on screen until you select one of the options. The ESCAPE key or CTRL-BREAK (CTRL-SCROLL LOCK) will also remove the Advanced menu.

BLOCK COMMANDS

In Quattro, special significance is attached to the word *block*, which refers to a single cell or any group of cells that forms a rectangular shape. This is directly equivalent to the term *range* as it is used in 1-2-3.

Many Quattro commands refer to blocks. They are defined by entering any two diagonally opposed coordinates for a group of cells, such as A1 through C5. Blocks can be defined by typing the coordinates or by pointing to them, using the cursor keys to move the cell selector. Quattro shows the coordinates separated by two periods, as in A1..C5. Block coordinates are said to be *anchored* when they are connected by these periods. Cell coordinates can be unlocked by pressing the ESCAPE key. This leaves the first coordinate, which can be changed by moving the cell selector. The coordinate can be reanchored by typing one period. Using BACKSPACE to unlock coordinates places the cell selector in the cell it occupied when the command requiring the coordinates was issued.

/Block Copy

The /Block Copy command is one of the most powerful in Quattro's repertoire. With it you can replicate numbers, labels, and formulas. The cell references in formulas are adjusted relative to their new location, unless they have been fixed as absolute references (A1 is a relative reference, A1 is an absolute reference). The protection status of a cell, as well as any format assigned to the cell by the /Block Display Format command, is also copied. Column width settings are not changed. The /Block Copy command can reproduce one cell into another or one cell into many cells; it can duplicate a group of cells one time or many times.

The /Block Copy command requires you to specify a source block of cells and then a destination for the copy. Normally, the source block will be the cells containing the entries you want copied. The destination will be the top-left cell of the area into which you want the copy or copies of the source cell(s) to be placed. If there is just one source cell but many destination cells, multiple copies of the source are produced. If the data to be copied occupies several cells, only one copy of the source block is placed in the destination. However, if you include blank cells in the source block, you can produce multiple copies of multiple cells. For example, if you specify A1..A14 as the source block when there is data in cells A1 and A2 only, and you then specify

A3 as the destination, you will produce seven copies of A1 and A2, occupying cells A3 through A16. Data in a destination area will be overwritten by the copied data unless the destination area is protected.

Tips When the source block and destination are the same, the /Block Copy command simply calculates formulas in the block. This enables you to set the default calculation method to Manual and then calculate just one area of the spreadsheet separately from rest.

You will use the /Block Copy command extensively when you are building spreadsheet models. The rhythm of the command keys will become second nature. To copy one cell to many cells, the pattern is /Block Copy, ENTER, anchor, point, ENTER. To copy from many cells to one destination, use /Block Copy, point, ENTER, point, ENTER. When copying a block of several cells to multiple locations, use /Block Copy, point, ENTER, anchor, point, ENTER. If you wish, you can use a shortcut feature to assign /Block Copy to a single keystroke such as CTRL-C. Just press / and select Block. You then highlight the Copy option on the Block menu and then press CTRL-ENTER. You will be prompted for a CTRL key to use. Press CTRL-C and from now on you will be able to use that keystroke as a shortcut to commence the /Block Copy command.

The /Block Copy command does not check for existing data in the destination cells. You can actually lose data by inadvertently copying over it. Usc caution the first fcw times you use this command, and always save the worksheet as a precaution before large /Block Copy operations.

/Block Move

The /Block Move command allows you to rearrange data that has already been entered into a spreadsheet. The contents of a cell or cells are transferred to a new location. The contents are not changed in relation to their new location; however, when data that is referenced by other cells is moved, Quattro updates those cell references. Similarly, if you move a block that is self-contained (that is, comprised of values and a formula that depends only on those values being moved), then the formula is updated based on the new location of the data.

The /Block Move command requires as input the source block of cells that are to be moved and the destination for the cells. You need only specify the top-left corner of the destination area. Data in the dcstination area will be overwritten by the moved data unless the destination area is protected.

Tips Watch for the effects of the /Block Move command, since it does change cell references in your spreadsheet. If you have the formula +A1+A2 stored in A3 and you move that formula to B5, it will still read +A1+A2. The same calculation is still being performed; it is just stored in a different location. If you were to move the data in A1 and A2 to B1 and B2, the formula would be updated to read +B1+B2 whether or not the formula has been moved. The /Block Move command also changes absolute references in a worksheet if you move a formula containing an absolute reference to a new location, or if you move a cell that is referenced absolutely.

If you move a block of cells that has been assigned a block name or contains within it a named cell or cells, the block name remains attached to the cells, and the coordinates of the block name are updated.

/Block Erase

The /Block Erase command offers a convenient way to delete the contents of a group of cells. Formats assigned to cells with the /Block Display Format command are not changed and /Block Erase will not remove the contents of protected cells. Formulas elsewhere in the spreadsheet that refer to data in cells that are erased are not changed, but can result in 0 or ERR depending on the type of formula.

The /Block Erase command requires you to indicate a block of cells to be modified. These are the cells whose contents will be removed, not columns and rows that will be taken out of the worksheet.

Tips /Block Erase does not remove block names assigned to cells within the block that is modified. To remove a block name, you must use the /Block Advanced Delete command.

While /Block Erase is best for removing the contents of several cells at once, the DEL key is quicker for deleting single cells.

/Block Display Format

The /Block Display Format command changes the way in which values are displayed and printed out. A format is assigned to a cell or group of cells, and this format is different from the global or default format. A format code is visible in the cell descriptor line when you are viewing a cell formatted with the /Block Display Format command.

To use the /Block Display Format command, you must choose which format you want and, in some cases, the number of decimal places to be shown; you must also specify the block to be modified. The available formats are Fixed, Scientific, Currency, Financial (,), General, +/-, Percent, Date (including Time), Text (Show

Formulas), and Hidden. These formats are listed and described in the table at the end of this guide, along with the codes used in the cell descriptor line to identify them. You can also select Reset from the Block Display Format menu, which returns a cell's format to the current default format.

Tips Cells formatted separately from the default format are not affected by changes to the default format. If you make a change to the overall format by using the /Default Formats Display command and the command does not appear to take effect, check the cell descriptor line while you are viewing cells and determine if they have been separately formatted. You can return all cells in a spreadsheet to their defaults by using the /Block Display Format Reset command and defining the block to be modified as A1 through the end of the spreadsheet, reached by END HOME.

A format assigned to a cell by means of the /Block Display Format command is copied along with the data in the cell when you use the /Block Copy command. Formatting cells before copying them can save a lot of work.

/Block Label Align

The /Block Label Align command offers you a way to change the alignment labels in a block of cells. For example, it would allow you to center all of the names in a row or right align all the names in a column. The command only changes the alignment of existing labels.

To use /Block Label Align, you specify Left, Right, or Center alignment. You must then indicate the block of cells to be modified.

/Block Fill

The /Block Fill command produces a column or row of sequential values. You can use it to number lists, create a range of values, generate a series of dates, and so on.

The /Block Fill command requires a destination for the series of numbers—a block of cells large enough to accommodate the full range of numbers you are creating; a start value, which is the beginning value in the series; a step value, which is the size of the increment between values; and a stop value, which is the last number in the series or a number beyond values that will fill the destination. Default settings are 0 for the start value, 1 for the step value, and 8192 for the stop value. The start value can be a number or a formula. The step value can be a positive or a negative number. The stop value does not have to be exactly the last number in the series if you simply want to fill all of the destination cells. If the step value is positive, the stop value should be greater than the start value. If the step value is negative, the stop value should be less than the start value; otherwise, Quattro will not fill the destination area.

Tips You can fill both columns and rows, or a combination of both. Thus, with A1..B20 as the destination, a start value of 100, a step value of 10, and a stop value of 8192, Quattro would place the numbers 100 through 290 in cells A1 through A20 and the numbers 300 through 490 in the cells B1 through B20.

You can create a series of dates (for example, 30-day periods that would begin on January 1, 1989) by using @DATE(89,1,1) as the starting value and formatting the destination cells with the /Block Display Format Date command.

To add a column of sequential numbers to a database, use the /Block Fill command and include the column in the sort block to allow reordering of the database to its original sequence.

/Block Search/Replace

The /Block Search/Replace command offers a powerful means of searching for any string of characters occurring anywhere in a block of cells, replacing that string with a different string, or removing it by replacing it with nothing.

The /Block Search/Replace command requires a block of cells to be searched, a search string that is to be found, a replace string that is to be substituted for the searched string, a Go command to initiate the process, and a Quit command to clear the menu if you do not proceed with the search.

When you use the Go command, you will either hear a beep indicating that what you were searching for does not exist in the search block, or you will be shown the contents of the first cell within the block that contains the search string, together with a menu of choices. Select Yes to replace this instance of the string; No to skip this instance and leave the cell unchanged; All to complete the search/replace operation, automatically changing all instances; or Quit to terminate the search/replace action and leave the currently indicated cell unchanged. You can use the ESCAPE key instead of Quit to terminate the search/replace action.

Tip You can change elements of formulas as well as labels with the Search/Replace feature. All instances of @SUM could be changed to @AVG. All instances of the @DATE(88,1,1) entry could also be changed to @DATE(89,1,1). You can shorten the target string, as in TE(88 instead of @DATE(88,1,1), but be sure to include enough of the string to make it unambiguous (not just 8, but 88).

/Block Reformat

The /Block Reformat command is used to rearrange long text entries into a series of shorter labels of equal width. Since Quattro will permit you to enter labels of up to 256 characters, you can type several sentences of text at once. However, Quattro will not perform word wrap as you type. Instead, you make a normal-appearing piece text out of long labels, using the /Block Reformat command. This command does not split words and so performs a primitive form of word wrap. The command will not work on long labels that are continuous strings of characters, such as decorative lines.

The /Block Reformat command requires a block of cells to be modified. If this block is just a single row of cells, Quattro will assume that it can use as many rows as are necessary to enter the successive lines of reformatted text. This can cause previously entered labels below the cell being reformatted to be incorporated at the end of the reformatted material, as well as the movement of value cells. If the block to be modified contains more than one row, it must contain enough rows to accommodate the reformatted text. Otherwise, you will get the message "Outp. block too small" and the command will be aborted.

Tip If you have to edit text that has been reformatted and end up with a line significantly shorter than the others, you can reissue the /Block Reformat command. This will rejustify the line, making it conform with the others.

BLOCK ADVANCED COMMANDS

When you select Advanced from the Block menu, there are four commands that allow you to transform and protect spreadsheet entries. The same menu lists the Block Name commands, discussed in the next section of this guide.

/Block Advanced Values

The /Block Advanced Values command converts a formula to its current value. The command operates like the /Block Copy command, except that any formulas in the copied data are turned into values in the new location.

The /Block Advanced Values command requires a source block of cells that contain the formulas you want to convert, and a destination for the converted data. If you make the destination different from the source block, you will have two versions of the same data: the original, which remains dynamic formulas, and the copy, which is static values. If you make the destination identical to the source block, you will have permanently converted dynamic formulas to static values.

Tip To convert a single cell from a formula to a value, use the F2 (Edit) key followed by the F9 (Calc) key and then press ENTER. This edits the cell contents, converts them to a value, and reenters them in the same cell.

► /Block Advanced Transpose

The /Block Advanced Transpose command allows you to rotate a collection of data so that what was in rows will be in columns, and what was in columns will be in rows. The command acts as a variation of the /Block Copy command, placing a rotated copy of cells into the worksheet.

The /Block Advanced Transpose command requires a source block of cells that are to be rotated and a destination for the rotated data to appear in the worksheet. These two areas should be separate; otherwise, part of the data will be overwritten.

Tip Use this command to prepare Quattro data for export to a database program such as Paradox, Reflex, or dBASE. To translate data to such programs, your spreadsheet data must be in rows that represent records and fields that represent fields. Similarly, data imported from such programs to Quattro can be transposed after translation in order to fit you spreadsheet design.

/Block Advanced Protect

The /Block Advanced Protect command is used to change the protection status of cells. If you have protected an entire worksheet with /Default Protection Enable and then removed protection from a cell with /Block Advanced Unprotect, you can use /Block Advanced Protect to reprotect the cell. Also, if you have turned off global protection with /Default Protection Disable, you can return specifically unprotected cells to normal status with the /Block Advanced Protect command.

The /Block Advanced Protect command requires a block of cells to be modified. The modified cells will bear the code PR (for protected) in the cell descriptor if Default Protection is enabled.

/Block Advanced Unprotect

The /Block Advanced Unprotect command is used to change the protection status of cells. If you have protected an entire worksheet with /Default Protection Enable, you can remove protection from a specific cell or group of cells with /Block Advanced Unprotect. You can use the /Advanced Database Form Input command to restrict cell selector movement to a block of unprotected cells.

The /Block Advanced Unprotect command requires a block of cells to be modified. The modified cells will bear the code U (which stands for unprotected) in the cell descriptor.

Tip Unprotected cells can be displayed with colors or attributes that are different from those of normal cells in order to make them easier to identify. Use the /Default Colors Spreadsheet Unprotected command to do this.

BLOCK NAME COMMANDS

When you select Advanced from the Block menu, you will see five commands headed Block Name: Create, Delete, Labels, Reset, and Make Table.

► /Block Advanced Create

The /Block Advanced Create command attaches a name to a cell or group of cells. The cell or cells can then be referred to by that name in formulas, menu settings, cursor movement, and macros.

The /Block Advanced Create command requires a name to create or modify and a block of cells to which the name will be attached. The name can be up to 15 characters, unique within the worksheet, and must not be the same as a cell coordinate. Naming a block P88 would be confusing, since there is also a cell called P88. (88P would be acceptable, as would "P88" with the quotes as part of the name). Any characters are acceptable in block names, but Quattro will not differentiate between upper- and lowercase letters in a name; SALES, Sales, and sales will all be recorded as the same name and listed as SALES. One cell can be in several different-named blocks, and you can assign more than one name to an identical block of cells. These other names are thought of as synonyms for the original name.

Tips Use block names such as Print Block and Sort Block instead of cell coordinates in formulas and settings. They are easier to remember and easier to type correctly.

You can move to the top-left corner of any named block by using the F5 key and the block name. The F3 key can be used to list the names from which to choose.

/Block Advanced Delete

The /Block Advanced Delete command removes block names. It does not remove the cells to which the name refers or delete the contents of those cells.

The /Block Advanced Delete command requires a name to remove. An alphabetical list of existing names from which to choose is displayed. Highlight the name to be removed, and press ENTER. A wide version of the Block Name list is visible when you press the gray plus key (Expand). You can type in the name instead of selecting one from the list, but if you type a nonexistent name, an error will result and the command will be aborted.

Tip If you need to remove most of the block names you have assigned, you may want to use the /Block Advanced Reset command, which deletes all block names.

/Block Advanced Labels

The /Block Advanced Labels command offers a convenient way to assign names to cells. The block name is typed in a cell adjacent to the actual cell that is to be named.

The /Block Advanced Labels command requires you to specify the relationship of the label that is going to be used as a block name to the cell it is going to name, either Right, Down, Left, or Up; it also requires the location of the cell or cells containing the labels. You can type a series of labels in a row and use those labels to name the cell below them by means of the Down option, indicating the row of names as the source of the labels. Quattro will simply ignore empty cells in the block of labels.

/Block Advanced Reset

The /Block Advanced Reset command offers you a quick way to remove all block name assignments.

The /Block Advanced Reset command requires that you reply Yes or No to the prompt "Delete all Named Blocks?" with No as the default choice. Pressing ESCAPE or ENTER at this point is the same as saying No.

Tip Do not use this command lightly. If you have set the Borland style confirmation option to No with the /Default Startup Compatibility Options command, you will not get a chance to say No here.

/Block Advanced Make Table

The /Block Advanced Make Table command places a list of block names and their coordinates into a worksheet. Quattro does show you existing block names when you use the /Block Advanced Create command, and also shows you their coordinates if you use the wide version of the menu. For a more permanent record of block names, use the /Block Advanced Make Table command.

To use the /Block Advanced Make Table command, you must indicate the upper-left cell of the area on the spreadsheet into which you want Quattro to place the information. The data takes up two columns and one row for each name. Be aware that this is data destructive—that is, it will overwrite data in unprotected cells if it needs the room to list all the names.

Tips This command does not create a dynamic table—it is not updated automatically. You must use the /Block Advanced Make Table command each time you want a current listing.

A more convenient method for viewing names than the /Block Advanced Make Table command is the F3 key, which displays a list of names. This list can also be expanded to show coordinates.

COLOR COMMANDS

When you select Color from the Default menu, you are able to specify Quattro's display colors for color monitors and display attributes for monochrome monitors. The available colors depend upon the type of display adapter you are using. The monochrome attributes are Normal, Bold, Underlined, Inverse, and Empty.

► /Default Colors Menu

The /Default Colors Menu command changes the colors used to display Quattro menus.

This command requires you to specify the area you want to change. The options are Frame, Banner, Text,

Key Letter, Highlight, Settings, Explanation, or Drop Shadow.

/Default Colors Spreadsheet

The /Default Colors Spreadsheet command changes the colors used to display the Quattro spreadsheet.

This command requires that you choose the area you want to affect. The options are Borders, Cells, Titles, Highlight, Descriptor Line, Status Line, Input Line, Unprotected, Labels, or Error Messages.

/Default Colors Conditional

The /Default Colors Conditional command sets colors for cells that will vary depending upon certain conditions in those cells. A set of conditional cell colors can be stored but disabled when appropriate.

The /Default Colors Conditional command requires that you enable or disable the use of conditional colors with the On/Off option. The conditional settings you can modify are ERR, Smallest Normal Value, Greatest Normal Value, Below Normal Color, Normal Cell Color, and Above Normal Color.

/Default Colors Palettes

The /Default Colors Palettes command reinstates a standard set of display colors. It offers a simple way to return the color settings to the original defaults.

The /Default Colors Palettes command requires that you choose between Color, Monochrome, and Black & White. The appropriate choice will depend upon your monitor.

/Default Colors Help

The /Default Colors Help command changes the colors used to display Quattro menus.

This command requires you to specify the area you want to change. The options are Banner, Text, Keywords, or Highlight.

/Default Colors Quit

The /Default Colors Quit command offers a quick means of exiting from the color menu to Ready mode. This allows you to view the changes you have made. Each submenu of the Colors menu also has a Quit option that provides the same feature.

The /Default Colors Quit command does not require input, but you must use the /Default Update command to store the current color choices to the configuration file. Otherwise, Quattro will revert to the previous settings in the next session. Pressing ESCAPE instead of selecting Quit will return you to the main Default menu.

COLUMN COMMANDS

This section discusses the commands used when working with columns.

/Column Insert

The /Column Insert command offers a quick way to add one or more new columns to a spreadsheet. Columns are inserted to the left of the current cell. Other columns are relettered, and cell references in formulas are updated automatically. Named blocks and block settings are expanded to include the new columns when the cell selector is in any column of the block except the leftmost column prior to the /Column Insert command being issued. The width of the new columns is determined by the current global width setting.

To use the /Column Insert command, you must identify the position of the column(s) to be inserted. To inset one column to the left of the cell your selector occupies, simply press ENTER. To insert more than one column, press the left or right arrow key once for each additional column. You can use the up or down arrow key to scan areas of the spreadsheet beyond the current view to make sure that the insert action will not disrupt existing work. You can press ESCAPE to unlock the location of the current cell and move the cell selector to another location prior to completing the command if you wish.

Tip If you have data in all 256 columns from A to IV, you cannot insert any more columns.

/Column Delete

The /Column Delete command quickly removes one or more new columns from a spreadsheet. Other columns are relettered. The total size of the spreadsheet area is not reduced, since new empty columns are added at the right edge of the worksheet.

The /Column Delete command requires you to identify the columns to be deleted. You can move the selector around to view other parts of the column than those currently in view, thereby making sure that you do not accidentally delete data.

/Column Width

The /Column Width command gives you a way to set the width of the current column. Column widths are measured in characters, and they can be from 1 to 240 characters wide. Widths set by the /Column Width command will not change when the global or default width is altered. A width code that displays the current width set with this command is shown in the descriptor line for all cells in the column. Cell widths cannot vary within a column.

To use the /Column Width command, enter the width either by typing a number and pressing ENTER, or use the left or right arrow key to change the width one character at a time so that you can view the new width on screen before pressing ENTER.

► /Column Reset

The /Column Reset command allows you to "undo" the /Column Width command and let the width of a column revert to the global width setting.

This command requires you to place your cell selector in the column to be affected before you select the command. The command executes as soon as it is selected.

► /Column Hide

The /Column Hide command removes columns from view, while allowing them and the data they contain to remain active within the spreadsheet.

This command requires you to indicate the columns to be hidden. The letters of the hidden columns are not shown in the top border of the spreadsheet, and the cell selector cannot enter them in Ready mode. During the operation of some commands, such as /Block Erase, the hidden columns are revealed to make sure their contents are considered during the command's execution. Hidden columns that are temporarily revealed are marked by an asterisk next to the column letter in the top border.

Tip Avoid drastic rearrangement of spreadsheet data for print or display purposes by hiding unnecessary columns. The formulas and data within the hidden columns will remain active, so this command will not affect spreadsheet accuracy.

► /Column Expose

The /Column Expose command is used to reveal hidden columns.

This command requires you to indicate which columns you want to expose. The hidden columns are revealed with asterisks marking them so that you can select them. To expose a single column, place your cell selector in that column and press ENTER. To expose several connected columns, you can type a period to anchor your cell selector in the first column of the group and use your arrow keys to include other columns before pressing ENTER. To expose several unconnected hidden columns, you will need to repeat the command.

/Column Set Global

The /Column Set Global command allows you to set the width of all columns in the spreadsheet that have not been individually set with the /Column Width command. This command is the same as the /Default Format Width of Column command; changes in one are reflected in the other.

To use the /Column Set Global command, either type the width in characters or use the left or right arrow keys to contract or expand the width on the screen of columns that have not been set. Pressing ENTER changes the width of all existing unset columns and provides a default width for new columns added by the /Column Insert command. Individually set columns will revert to the current global setting when you use the /Column Reset command.

DATABASE COMMANDS

A *database* is a collection of pieces of information arranged in a meaningful way. A name and address list or a library catalog file is a database. All of the information about one entity (a person or book, for example) is a *record*. The categories into which the record is divided (first name, last name, address, title, and so on) are *fields*. Quattro can sort and filter a collection of information if it is arranged in a table with each row as a record and each field as a column. The records must occupy contiguous rows and the fields contiguous columns, usually headed by field names.

/Advanced Database Sort

The /Advanced Database Sort command rearranges lists of data in the spreadsheet according to alphabetical or numeric order. You can sort a name and address list by last name or by ZIP code. You are allowed up to five sort keys or levels of sort, so you can sort by last name, first name, middle initial, city, and state. You can sort any column of consecutive cell entries, even if they were not designed as a database.

The /Advanced Database Sort command requires you to make several settings before you select the Go command. You can use the Reset option to erase these settings. You can also use the Sort Order option to change the sort priority of labels versus numbers and the order of alphabetical sorting between Dictionary (Aa Bb..Zz) and ASCII (AB..Z..ab..z). The settings are as follows: Sort Block, which are the cells occupied by the data to be sorted (this is all of the fields of all of the records, but not the field names); Keys (1st, 2nd, 3rd, 4th, and 5th), which means the first cell of each of the columns or fields upon which the sort will be based; and Ascending or Descending order for each key selected.

Tip You should sort all columns of the database at once. Identify the sort block by using the END and arrow keys to be sure that all data is included. Save your file before sorting. Use a block name for the sort block. The term *Ascending* means a numerical order of 1,2,3, alphabetical order of A,B,C, and age ordered from oldest to youngest.

/Advanced Database Query

The /Advanced Database Query locates database records that meet specific criteria and also extracts lists of such data.

This command requires you to make certain settings, such as the location of the database and your criteria (the target of your query), before you use the Locate option to find records meeting your criteria, the Extract option to list the target data, or the Delete option to remove target data. The settings can be reset with the Reset option.

The settings are as follows:

- Query Block to indicate the cells contained in the database, including the field-name row.
- Assign Names to automatically block name the first data cell in each column with the name of the field, using the field-name label. This

allows you to refer to the field in a Formula Criterion such as PRICE > 30.

- Formula Criterion to enter a criterion in formula format, using a field name and an operator and a value, as indicated on the prompt line.
- Criteria Table to indicate cells on the spreadsheet containing one or more field names and below them the values being sought in the respective fields.
- Output Block to indicate an area of the spreadsheet in which a row of field names has been entered, one for each field that is to be listed by the Extract option.

The Locate option initially highlights the first row in the query block that meets the criterion. You can move the cursor across the row to each column and press F2 to edit any field of that record. You can use the down arrow key to move the highlighting to the next record that meets the criteria, until there are no more records and Quattro beeps. Press ESCAPE or CTRL-BREAK (SCROLL LOCK) to leave the Locate operation. You can repeat the last Locate operation from Ready mode by pressing the F7 key. Escaping from a Locate operation initiated in this way returns you to Ready mode. Escaping from a Locate operation performed from the Query menu returns you to the menu. Using

CTRL-BREAK to exit a Locate operation always returns you to Ready mode.

The Extract option sends matching data into the output block from the database, according to the criteria and the field names you have entered in the output block. You can report just a few fields of information about the matching records, or all of the fields. The output fields can be different from the criteria fields. Be sure that the output block is defined to include enough room for matching records but is not defined so that the records overlap existing data, which could be overwritten. Sending data with incorrect criteria can cause all records to be output.

The Delete option removes records that meet a certain criterion by deleting the cells they occupy. Although Quattro will warn you before deleting records, be sure to check that the criterion for a Delete operaion is correct by first performing a Locate operation. Delete does not remove data from cells outside of the query block.

The Unique option performs the same action as the Extract option, except that duplicate records are only output once. You can use this option to remove duplicate data from the database if you define the output block as the query block and use a criterion that finds all records. Any identical records are found, and just one is retained.

/Advanced Database Form Input

The /Advanced Database Form Input command restricts the movement of the cell selector to a certain area of the worksheet. This can help operators to enter data in the spreadsheet.

To use the /Advanced Database Form Input command, you must identify the area in which movement will be limited. This area must coincide with an unprotected block in an otherwise protected spreadsheet. Pressing ESCAPE while in Ready mode will unlock this command and allow movement anywhere on the spreadsheet.

/Advanced Database Quit

The /Advanced Database Quit command offers a quick way to return to Ready mode.

This command's only requirement is that you must select it.

DEFAULT COMMANDS

The defaults of a computer program are what the program assumes you would like it to do and the choices you would like it to make for you. The /Default command provides access to eight areas of Quattro's operation. You can change the default settings for Hardware,

Colors, International, Formats, Directories, Recalculation, Protection, and Startup. Three of these areas—Formats, Recalculation and Protection—relate principally to the current worksheet, while the five other areas affect the ongoing operation of the program beyond the current session. There are two other options on the Default menu: Update, which records the current default settings in a configuration file, and Quit, which returns you to Ready mode.

Since Quattro automatically installs itself on most personal computers, detecting the kind of equipment present and adjusting to it, there is really no installation process for the program. However, to customize such aspects as display colors and spreadsheet storage areas, you will want to use the /Default command. The various parts of the /Default command are treated separately in this guide under these command headings: Directories Commands, Formats Commands, Hardware Commands, International Commands, Protection Commands, Recalculation Commands, Startup Commands, and Update Commands.

DIRECTORIES COMMANDS

Which disk drive you use for program or data storage, and which directory area you use within a disk, is related to Quattro through the Directories commands.

► /Default Directories Resource

The /Default Directories Resource command allows you to let Quattro know where the system files are being stored.

This command requires you to enter the appropriate drive and directory information.

► /Default Directories Data

The /Default Directories Data command allows you to let Quattro know where to look for data files.

This command requires you to enter the appropriate drive and directory information.

► /Default Directories Quit

The /Default Directories Quit command offers a quick way out of the Directories menu, back to Ready mode.

This command's only requirement is that you must select it.

ERASE COMMAND

The /Erase command is used to clear the current worksheet from memory in preparation for creating a new worksheet.

The /Erase command requires careful attention. It clears your entire worksheet area—all 2 million plus cells. To help prevent the accidental erasure of unstored work, Quattro watches for any changes to the worksheet since the last time it was saved. If no changes are detected, the /Erase command will execute immediately. If changes are detected, you will be asked if you want to save them. You should respond with Yes to complete the command, with No to cancel the command, or press ESCAPE, which is the same as No.

FILE COMMANDS

This section describes commands used when working with files.

/File Retrieve

The /File Retrieve command is used to bring a copy of a file from the disk into memory and into the worksheet area. This command will retrieve files created by other programs. Files other than Quattro files are translated into Quattro format. All information currently in the worksheet area is overwritten when a file is retrieved.

The /File Retrieve command requires extreme caution. You are not told whether your current work has been saved before another worksheet overwrites it.

/File Save

The /File Save command is used to store worksheets on disk.

This command requires you to specify the filename, up to eight letters, numbers, and certain punctuation characters (those characters allowed include !, @, #, $, %, ^, &, -, _, ', {, }, \, /, and ~). The filename extension will determine the file format of the stored data. Using .WKQ results in a Quattro format file. Both .WKS and .WK1 can be used to store data in Lotus 1-2-3 Release 1 and 2 format. The SQZ! option is activated by using .WKZ to create a compressed Quattro file.

Tip Unless you type in a specific filename extension, the default extension will be used. You set the default extension with the /Default Startup Extension command. The extension is initially .WKQ. Other SQZ! extensions include .WK$ (for Release 1) and .WK! (for Release 2) for compressed 1-2-3 files. Use .WRK to store a file that is readable by Symphony, .RXD for files that are readable by Reflex, .DB for Paradox, .DB2 for dBASE II, and .DBF for dBASE III. When using database file extensions (.RXD, .DB, .DB2, or .DBF), you will be prompted to review structure and to check if the file translation feature has correctly interpreted the file names, file lengths, data types, and formats.

/File Combine

The /File Combine command allows you to copy a file into the current worksheet without completely erasing the existing data. The occupied cells of the incoming file overwrite existing cells, but empty cells in the incoming file do not blank out already occupied cells.

To use the /File Combine command, place your cell selector in the top-left corner of the area in which you would like the files combined. Then choose between having the incoming data copied into the current worksheet (Copy), added to the existing values in the worksheet (Add), or subtracted from the current values (Subtract). You must then choose between combining an entire file (File) or a specific block of cells (Block), which you indicate with a set of coordinates or a block name. Finally, you must indicate the name of the file that is being combined.

\File Import

The /File Import command allows data from other programs to be read into Quattro. Programs whose data cannot be read directly into Quattro with the /File Retrieve command can still send data to Quattro by printing it to a disk file. This creates an ASCII file. Sometimes data in this file can be organized for easier reading by use of commas and quotes separating numbers and labels. Such a file is called a *delimited* file.

The /File Import command requires you to place your cell selector in the top-left corner of the area in which you would like the data to be placed. You then tell Quattro whether the file to be imported is an ASCII file or a delimited file. You are then shown a list of all files in the current directory that have the .PRN extension. You can search other directories and look for different extensions. Having specified the file name, you press ENTER. The data is read from the file into the spreadsheet. If the data is delimited, it will be arranged in columns and rows. If it is not delimited, it will be a series of long labels in the current column. You can split long labels of data into separate cells with string functions or the /File Parse command.

/File Xtract

The /File Xtract command gives you a way to save part of a spreadsheet to disk.

To use this command, you must first decide between extracting formulas or values. You then specify the name of the file into which the extracted data will be stored. If a file of that name already exists, you will have an opportunity to cancel the use of that name or replace the previous file. You then indicate the block of cells to be extracted.

Tip When you increase a spreadsheet to the point where your system's memory is full, you can store separate parts of the large spreadsheet to different files and then delete the original parts to make the current spreadsheet more manageable.

/File Erase

The /File Erase command is used to remove files from disk.

This command requires you to specify the type of file you want to erase.The type of file you select will determine which files are listed for you to pick from. Choosing Worksheet will show .WK? files, Printing will show .PRN files, Graph will show .PIC files, and Other will show all files. Highlight the file to be erased on the file list, and press ENTER. You will need to confirm the erase when you see the Yes/No prompt.

/File Directory

The /File Directory command temporarily changes the area to which Quattro looks for data files. Quattro reverts to the default data directory when you reload it.

The /File Directory command requires you to enter the name of the directory. It then returns you to Ready mode.

/File Parse

The /File Parse command is used to divide data that is simply a series of long labels into separate cells, usually after data has been imported from an ASCII file with the /File Import command.

To use this command, you must create a format line that defines how the long labels will be split into separate cells. You can do this by placing your cell selector on the first of the labels before issuing the /File Parse command. This line can then be edited with the Edit option to make sure that it is correctly reading the data. The column of labels to be parsed are identified by the Input setting, and an area for the results of the parsing action is defined by the Output setting. When you pick Go, the labels indicated in the Input setting will be divided according to the settings on the format line and the data placed in the Output area. The parse settings can be reset with the /File Parse Reset command.

/File !SQZ!

The /File !SQZ! command "fine tunes" the settings of the !SQZ! program that is built into Quattro. The !SQZ! program compresses your spreadsheet files as they are stored, resulting in disk-space savings of up to 95%. You activate the !SQZ! feature when you are using the /File Save Command.

To use the /File !SQZ! command, you must select choices for the way !SQZ! will work. You can set the Remove Blanks option to Yes to increase the amount by which the file is reduced. You can set Storage of Values to Exact, Approximate, or Remove.The Exact setting does not affect values at all. The Approximate setting reduces the number of decimal places stored from 15 to 9. The Remove setting takes out values created by formulas and saves considerable space. The values are recalculated when the spreadsheet is retrieved. The Version option lets you choose between regular SQZ! and SQZ! Plus.

/File OS

The /File OS command allows you to temporarily suspend operation of Quattro and provides access to DOS commands. Use this command to return to the DOS prompt without having to use Quit to exit from Quattro. This is convenient for file operations, formatting new disks, making new directories, and so on. Do not run any programs that affect memory status while you are using /File OS; otherwise, Quattro may not be able to resume operation.

To use the /File OS command, you simply select it. You will have to type **EXIT** and press ENTER at the DOS prompt to return to Quattro.

FORMAT COMMANDS

This section describes the default format settings available in Quattro.

/Default Formats Display

The /Default Formats Display command sets the format used for the display of values in all cells not affected by a /Block Display Format command. The choice you make in this menu affects the current worksheet and all new worksheets created to the end of the current session. If you use the /Default Update command, then the /Default Formats Display choice will be recorded and will remain in effect in future Quattro sessions.

The /Default Formats Display command requires you to choose the format you want. The possible choices are listed at the end of this guide.

/Default Formats Align

The /Default Formats Align command allows you to change the label indicator that is always placed at the front of labels as you create them. Normally, this is the ' symbol, for a left-aligned label, but it can be changed to the ^ symbol for a centered label and " for a right-aligned label.

The /Default Formats Align command requires you to choose between Left, Right, and Centered.

Tip This command does not affect labels that have already been entered—only new labels. Use /Block Label Align to change the alignment of existing labels.

/Default Formats Hide Zeroes

The /Default Formats Hide Zeroes command hides from view any zeroes that appear in cells. This is useful when you have a great many formulas resulting in 0 until a key value is entered. However, you must be careful not to delete such cells simply because they appear empty. Their contents are visible on the descriptor line.

The /Default Formats Hide Zeroes command simply requires you to pick Yes or No.

/Default Formats Width of Column

The /Default Formats Width of Column command is the same as the /Column Set Global command.

This command requires that you indicate the desired width and press ENTER.

/Default Formats Clock

The /Default Formats Clock command removes the clock display from the lower left of the screen or changes the format of the date and time that it displays.

This command requires that you select Standard (25-Dec-89), International (the current setting for Long International, as in 25/12/89), or None.

/Default Formats Quit

The /Default Formats Quit command offers a quick way out of the /Default Formats menu and back to Ready mode.

This command's only requirement is simply that you select it.

FREQUENCY COMMANDS

The Frequency commands are used to perform a frequency distribution analysis on spreadsheet data; they report on how many items fall within a specified range of values. You can analyze a price list to see how many items fall into certain price ranges. You tell Quattro where the data to be analyzed is and what ranges of value to use.

When you select Frequency from the Advanced menu, you are asked to supply the location of a *values block*. This is the data that you want analyzed. When you have indicated this area you are prompted for a *bins block*. This is a column of cells into which you have entered the values by which you want your data categorized. The bin values 100, 500, 1000 would categorize the data values as less than or equal to 100, greater than 100 and up to and including 500, and greater than 500 and up to and including 1000. Upon entering the bins block, you will see a list of numbers in the column next to the block, reporting a count of how many values in the values block fall in the established ranges. If there are values greater than the large bin number, then they are counted in the cell below the last cell of the report column.

GRAPH COMMANDS

This section describes the commands used to create, view, save, and print graphs by using data in your worksheet.

/Graph Type

The /Graph Graph Type command is used to change the type of graph generated from the graphed values.

This command requires that you choose between the available types. They are Line, Bar, XY, Stacked-Bar,

Pie, 3 Dimensional Bar, Area, Rotated Bar, Markers, Combined Lines and Markers.

Tip You can see the same data in several different graph types once you have defined the X-axis and Y-axis. You will need to use a different set of data for a pie chart because it is one-dimensional (a pie chart uses the data from the 1st Series area to generate the pie).

/Graph X-Axis Values

The /Graph X-Axis Values command is used to indicate the data that will form the basis of the X-axis. This can be a series of labels or values in adjacent cells of a column or row.

This command only requires that you identify the block of cells.

/Graph Series Values

The /Graph Series Values command indicates the values that are to be graphed along the Y-axis and the X-axis. They must be values and not labels. You can graph up to six series of data at one time.

The /Graph Series Values command requires you to select each of the six series in turn and identify the cells containing the values to be graphed.

/Graph Titles

The /Graph Titles command allows you to add explanatory titles to graphs.

This command requires you to enter the text you want to appear on the graph. This is divided into 1st Line and 2nd Line for centered headings, and X and Y for the two axes. The Size option can be used to select a size for the text in the titles; the Font option can be used to choose the style of characters for the text of the titles.

/Graph Customize

The /Graph Customize command is your key to a vast array of options that allow you to customize the graph created by the above settings.

To use this command, you must select which areas you want to customize: Series, X-Axis, Y-Axis, Colors, Pies, Resolution, or Grids.

The /Graph Customize Series options include Markers, Patterns, Legends, Interior Labels, and Override Type. You can also select each series individually and change the block, legend, interior labels, placement of labels, color, override type, markers, and fill pattern, as well as reset the series completely.

The /Graph Customize X-Axis options allow you to change the title of the axis; X values; the scale; the low value, high value, and increment value; the format of ticks, the number of minor ticks, and alternative ticks; and display scaling. You can also use Reset to erase the X-axis settings.

The /Graph Customize Y-axis options allow you to change the title of the axis; the scale; the low value, high value, and increment value; the format of ticks and the number of minor ticks; and display scaling. You can also use Reset to erase the Y-axis settings.

The /Graph Customize Colors options let you change the color of the series, the titles, the frame, the grid, and the background. You can also use the Update option to record these as the preferred choices for future sessions.

The /Graph Customize Pies options allow you to change a pie chart's label format, to explode certain sections, to change section patterns, and to modify section colors.

The /Graph Customize Resolution options allow you to modify the way your display shows graphs if you have several modes available. You can sometimes choose between different palettes of color, or different degrees of sharpness or resolution.

The /Graph Customize Grids options let you change the Color of a grid on the graph and the line type used in a grid. You can choose to frame the graph or not.

/Graph Reset

The /Graph Reset command changes the settings for any of the series of data or the X-axis. You can also reset all of the graph choices.

The /Graph Reset command requires you to select the series of data you want to reset, the X-axis option if that is what you want to change, or the Graph option if you want to completely redesign the graph.

/Graph Name

The /Graph Name command manages a collection of graphs. Only one graph at a time can be displayed by Quattro, just as a slide projector can only show one slide at a time. With the Display, Store Erase, and Reset options, the /Graph Name command moves graphs in and out of view. Once a graph has been created, it can be stored with the Store option and another graph brought forward with the Display option. Stored graphs can be erased with Erase, and all graph names can be wiped out with Reset.

To use the /Graph Name command, you choose Display, Store, Erase, or Reset. The first three options show you a list of current names from which to choose.

Tip Be sure to save your worksheet after you design a graph; otherwise, the settings will not be stored.

/Graph Print

The /Graph Print handles the printing of graphs. The graph that is printed is the one that was most recently displayed or most recently named with the /Graph Print Name option.

The /Graph Print command requires several pieces of information. The Printers setting is used to describe the printer or plotter on which the graph is to be printed. The Destination setting is used to specify which printer will be used or which file will store the graph for use by other programs. The Layout option is used to set the size and orientation of the graph on the paper. The Colors option is used to set colors for the various parts of the graph (this is applicable only for color output devices). The Colors option lets you copy the colors that are used in the graph as seen on screen. The Go option is used to initiate the print process. The Write EPS/PIC option is used to create special files to transfer graphs to other programs (a PIC file is compatible with 1-2-3 and an EPS with PostScript). The Name option calls up a named graph as the one to be printed (as opposed to the one most recently viewed). The Reset option resets the /Graph Print options, and the Update option records the settings for use in future sessions.

/Graph View

The /Graph View command allows you to view the current graph. (This comand will not work on systems using old IBM monochrome display adapters, but such systems can still print the graph.) There are View options on many of the Graph submenus to make it easy to see your progress in designing the graph.

The /Graph View command's only requirement is that you select it. Press any key while viewing a graph in order to return to the previous screen.

Tips You can view the current graph from Ready mode by using F10. If you press F10 and hear a beep, it means that no graph is currently defined. When you save a worksheet, the current graph is the one that will be current when next the file is retrieved.

Some elements of a graph's design may be hard to see because of color similarities. Use the /Graph Customize Colors command to change the colors in which the elements are displayed.

HARDWARE COMMANDS

This section describes commands you use to customize Quattro to work best with your computer hardware.

► /Default Hardware Screen

The /Default Hardware Screen command overrides Quattro's Autodetect feature, which senses what kind of display system you are using. You can adjust for different monitor types, different display adapters, and a second monitor.

The /Default Hardware Screen command is not necessary if your screen appears to be working properly. However, this command allows you to customize several items. If you have a black and white monitor connected to a color graphics adapter, you should select Color and choose No. (Compaq systems that emulate a CGA adapter with a monochrome display are correctly detected.)

Some color graphics adapters (other than Compaq) have a problem with screen flicker or snow when scrolling spreadsheets. Since not all CGAs have this problem, you can achieve faster display scrolling by setting Screen Snows to No. Change this option to Yes if a problem with scrolling appears. The Use Special Driver option is intended to allow as yet undeveloped display systems to work with Quattro.

Use the Graphic Screen option to specify a type for a second screen attached to your system. Use Resolution to select between different levels of resolution available on your hardware for graphics display; color graphics adapters can sometimes show sharper (higher resolution) images by limiting the number of different colors available. Use the Aspect Ratio option to adjust the way in which circles are displayed in pie charts. You will be shown a screen with a sample circle and instructed on how to make adjustments.

/Default Hardware Text Printer

The /Default Hardware Text Printer is used to fine-tune the interface between Quattro and the printer you use for spreadsheet (text) printing. You can change the port and specify continuous or single-sheet printing.

The /Default Hardware Text Printer command is not required if your printer is working properly when you are printing with the /Print command. You can use Device to choose between several parallel and serial ports or a postscript device. If you need to use a serial connection, you can specify baud, stop bits, and parity to match the printer. If you are getting unexpected double spacing on your printouts, you can change Auto LF to Yes. If you want to load paper a single sheet at a time, you can change the 1 Sheet setting to Yes. If you need to reset your printer before printing with Quattro, you can use the Reset option to store a setup string that is sent to the printer every time Quattro is loaded.

► Available Memory

The Available Memory option is not a command but a pair of statements specifying the amount of normal and expanded memory (EMS) that is installed in your system and used by Quattro. If you have EMS in your system but it is not detected by Quattro, check that the EMS software is installed correctly.

► Coprocessor

The Coprocessor option is not a command but a statement of whether or not Quattro has detected a coprocessor in your system. A coprocessor is an extra chip that helps the main processor to make math calculations much more quickly.

INTERNATIONAL COMMANDS

Quattro can be installed to handle a variety of foreign formats for such items as currency and dates.

/Default International Currency

The /Default International Currency command allows you to specify a character to be used in the Currency format instead of the $ symbol. You can have the symbol appear before or after the monetary figure.

To use the /Default International Currency command, you type a currency symbol and specify whether it is to be placed before the number (Prefix), as in $1,000, or after the number (Suffix), as in 1,000F. You can use any of the characters on the keyboard, as well as special ASCII characters if you refer to them by their decimal numbers. To enter an ASCII number as the currency symbol, hold down ALT and type the number on the numeric keypad (for example, 156 for the pounds sterling symbol).

/Default International Punctuation

The /Default International Punctuation command changes the punctuation used when formatting numbers, which allows you to conform to such foreign conventions as a comma for a decimal place and a period for thousand separator. You can also change the character used to separate arguments in a function statement. Instead of a comma, as in @SUM(A1..A4,B1..B4), you could specify a period or a semicolon.

The /Default International Punctuation command requires you to choose one of the eight different combinations of punctuation style.

/Default International Date

The /Default International Date command lets you change the date format used by Quattro whenever you specify International in a format menu.

To use this command, you must choose between MM/DD/YY, DD/MM/YY, DD.MM.YY, and YY.MM.DD formats. Whichever one you choose is the basis for both Long International and Short International in the block or default date format menus.

/Default International Time

The /Default International Time command allows you to change the format used by Quattro whenever you specify International in a time format menu.

This command requires that you choose one of the following standard formats: HH:MM:SS, HH.MM.SS, HH,MM,SS, and HHhMMmSSs. Whichever one you choose is the basis for both Long International and Short International in the block or default date format menus.

/Default International Quit

The /Default International Quit command offers a quick way back to Ready mode. Using the ESCAPE key instead of the Quit option will return you to the Default menu.

This command's only requirement is only that you select it.

LAYOUT COMMANDS

These commands are used to determine how a spreadsheet is presented.

/Layout Titles

The /Layout Titles command locks the cell selector out of an area of the spreadsheet that contains column and/or row headings. Freezing these headings on the screen makes it easier to read large spreadsheets. This command solves the problem of labels that head long columns of data scrolling off the top of the screen and leaving you uncertain as to which month of a one-year projection you are viewing, or which column of an inventory listing. It also solves the similar problem with row labels on wide models.

The /Layout Titles command requires you to place your cell selector in an appropriate position before the command, and then choose between titles that are horizontal, vertical or both. A Clear option is provided to remove a title setting. The Title option sets the title area above and to the left of the cell selector. A horizontal title simply freezes column headings; a vertical title freezes row headings. Column and row headings are frozen with the Both option.

/Layout Windows

The /Layout Windows command splits your screen, allowing you to see two parts of a spreadsheet at the same time.

To use this command, you must place your cursor in the column or row where you want the split to be made. You must choose between Horizontal and Vertical window options. When the window appears, you can move from one side to the other with the F6 key. Usually, the spreadsheet view in one window will be matched by movement in the other. However, you can use the Unsync option to prevent this, and thus move a completely separate area of the spreadsheet into one window. You can resynchronize windows with the Sync option. A window setting can be cleared with the Clear option.

/Layout Descriptor Line

The /Layout Descriptor Line command moves the descriptor line, which is usually one line from the bottom of the display, to the top of the screen, where it appears in 1-2-3.

This command only requires that you select it, and the line will move from the bottom to the top—or from the top to the bottom if it was already at the top. You are returned to the Layout menu after this command.

MACRO COMMANDS

Quattro provides excellent facilities for creating and using macros, which are stored keystrokes and commands that can be replayed at will to simplify repetitive actions and execute complex instructions.

/Macro Name

The /Macro Name command is another command for assigning a block name. Macro instructions are typed into cells as labels. For Quattro to execute these instructions, it must know where they are. This is usually done by means of a block name. There is no real limit to the number of names that can be used.

Some names are special. Macros named with the backslash and a single letter (\A through \Z) can be executed by holding down ALT and typing the letter. A macro named \0 will execute as soon as the spreadsheet in which it is stored is executed, as long as the default Startup Macro name is set to \0.

The /Macro Name command requires you to enter a name and indicate the cells to which it applies. You usually only name the first cell of a macro, since Quattro executes the instructions in that cell and then automatically reads the next cell below it for further instructions.

► /Macro Delete

The /Macro Delete command offers an alternative to the /Advanced Name Delete command.

This command's only requirement is that you select the name to be deleted from the list of existing names.

► /Macro Execute

The /Macro Execute command allows you to execute macro instructions by pointing to the cell in which they are stored. Quattro will then execute the instructions in that cell and look to the next cell down to see if there are any further instructions, and so on.

The /Macro Execute command requires the address of the first line of the macro you want to execute. This can be indicated by pointing, by typing the coordinates, by typing the name of a cell, or by pressing F3 and selecting the name from a list.

Tip This command is useful for executing part of a long macro without starting at the beginning and with-out bothering to name it. Simply point to the location within the macro at which you want to start.

▶ /Macro Clear Breakpoints

The /Macro Clear Breakpoints command is used with the Debugging feature to clear out all of the breakpoints and trace cells that were set up to help analyze the execution of a macro.

This command requires only that you issue it.

Quattro Add-Ins

Three commands on the Macro menu help you manage Quattro add-ins, programs that are not part of the Quattro program itself but are extra programs designed to work with Quattro. Two of these add-ins are shipped with Quattro. Thc Mcnu-Buildcr program allows you to customize the Quattro menu system. The Transcript program keeps a log of all your keystrokes and saves them to disk on a regular basis so that you can recover from a power failure, accidental /Block Erase, or some other catastrophe.

/Macro Load

The /Macro Load command connects add-ins with the main Quattro program.

To use this command, select the name of the desired add-in from a list of those available. If none are shown as available, check that they are stored in your resource directory. The files have the extension .QAI. The actions performed by the add-in after it is loaded depend upon its design. Some, like Transcript, immediately go to work when loaded. Others, like Menu-Builder, need to be activated by the /Macro Run command.

/Macro Run

The /Macro Run command activates add-in programs that have already been loaded. In the case of Transcript, this gives you access to the keystroke log. In the case of Menu-Builder, this command loads the entire current menu system into memory and presents a menu of editing options.

The /Macro Run command requires you to have first loaded the add-in. Loaded add-ins are listed for you to choose from.

/Macro Unload

The /Macro Unload command deactivates add-ins. You may want to use this command to free memory space when an add-in is no longer needed.

This command's only requirement is that you make a selection from the list of loaded add-ins.

MATRIX COMMANDS

These commands are used to multiply two matrices or to invert one matrix to create a second matrix.

/Advanced Matrix Multiply

The /Advanced Matrix Multiply command is used to multiply matrices of numbers.

This command requires you to specify the cells containing the first matrix of numbers, the second matrix of numbers, and a destination location for the result.

/Advanced Matrix Invert

The /Advanced Matrix Invert command inverts a matrix of numbers.

To use this command, specify the cells containing the numbers to be inverted and the location for the output of the inversion.

/Advanced Matrix Quit

The /Advanced Matrix Quit command offers a quick way to leave the Matrix menu and get back to Ready mode.

This command's only requirement is that you must select it.

MENU BUILDER COMMANDS

The entire Quattro menu structure is designed so that it can be easily redesigned. This means that you can make custom menus that are not worksheet-specific but system-specific.

The RSC Files

The system of menus that you access with the / key is stored in a file with the extension .RSC. When you use the /Default Startup Menu Tree command you see the current menu's tree file listed; QUATTRO.RSC is the default. This file is shipped with Quattro to supply the standard Quattro menus, but it can be copied and modified. A complete set of menus that are different from the standard Quattro menus is provided with the program. This is the file 123.RSC, which contains a menu system similar to that of 1-2-3.

To change from one menu system to another, you use the /Default Startup command and select Menu Tree. By selecting Main Menu, you will get a list of currently available menu files. You can select the one you want, and it will be placed in the Menus menu for you. Then you can select Update to write your choice of menu system to the configuration file.

When you exit from Quattro and reload the program, the new menu system you selected will be effect. In addition to the 123.RSC file that comes with Quattro, you can create your own .RSC file containing your own personalized menu system.

Running Menu Builder

To customize a menu system, you first need to load Menu Builder with the /Macro Load command. The actual program file is called MENUBLDR.QAI. Then select Menu Builder from the Macro Run list. You can do this while you have a spreadsheet loaded although memory constraints may make it easier to run Menu Builder with a blank work area.

When you choose to run Menu Builder, the program reads the current menu file into memory. The first item on the Menu Builder menu is Modify the Menus. Select this to change your menu system. The middle of the lower half of the next screen shows the main menu of your current menu system. There is a highlight bar that can be moved up and down the menu to highlight different items.

When an item is highlighted, the corresponding "child" menu is displayed on the right. Thus, the Block option on the main menu shows the Block menu to the right. You can move to the child menu with the right arrow key. Pressing the left arrow key moves you back to the parent menu. In the lower window you can perform cut and paste operations with the menu items to arrange them the way you want. Items can be deleted with the DELETE key. The remaining items will be regrouped to fill in the gap.

Using the upper window, you can customize an existing menu item or define a new one. You move from the lower part of the screen to the upper by pressing the Window key, F6. When you are in the upper window, you can edit any of the six pieces of information about the currently highlighted menu item. The first two categories in the upper window are the text of the menu and the explanation of the menu, which appears on the top line of the worksheet screen. The third category, Type of Action, refers to the way in which Quattro groups the commands. The Specific action refers to the actual act performed by the menu item, which may be nothing at all if the item leads to another menu. What to Do After Item Pressed determines the action performed after the menu item is selected.

The basic operation of cut and paste for menu items involves highlighting the menu item you want to move, pressing the DELETE key to remove it from the current menu, and then pressing the plus key to insert it when you have moved the highlight to the new location. The keys used are shown when you press F1 for the Menu Builder help screen.

New Items

If you want to add a new item to a menu, place the highlighting on the item above which you want the new one to appear, and press the INS key. A space opens up in the menu, and you are asked to name the item. When an item has been added, the Menu Text and Explanation fields in the upper window are set to match the item name. Type of Action is set to Basics and specific action is set to None. To specify the type of action, you can select an item from a list of possible actions. Just press any key while highlighting the Type of Action option entry and you get the list of the possible actions. The same feature helps you to select a Specific Action option. If the menu item itself performs no action other than to lead you to another menu, you enter None for the Specific Action option.

What to Do After Item Pressed is an option that controls the flow of the menu selection process and links one menu to another. The last field in the upper window is the Selectable Status field. This distinguishes between working menu items and those that are non-selectable (like Block Names).

New Branches

When you have completed the description of a new menu item, you can move back to the lower window. When you create a new item that leads to child menu, you automatically get a one item child. The single item is Quit, which many child menus contain anyway. Using the right arrow key to move to the child menu, you can begin to create new items on it. These can be designed items or existing items (like Default) moved from elsewhere in the menu system. To move a menu item like Default from one menu to another, you first delete it and then place the menu highlighting on the item above which you want to insert the option you just deleted. Press the plus key, and the last deleted item will be inserted, complete with all child menu connections. This makes it very easy to cut and paste whole branches of the menu tree.

Saving Menus

When you have made the desired changes to the menu structure you press ESCAPE to return to the Menu Builder menu. Here, you select Save Current Menu. This leads to a submenu that requests a choice between a normal and an alternate menu tree. In either case, you will be prompted for a file name. You can name it with any valid file name, up to eight characters. The extension .RSC will be attached to the file name. The new menu's tree file will usually be stored in the resource directory and needs to be in that directory for Quattro to be able to find the file to load the menu tree when it starts up.

When you make your choice of type and enter the new name, the program goes through three processes: analyzing, compressing, and saving. During each process the lower right of the screen shows a percentage countdown from 0% to 100% to let you know the progress of the program. When the new menu tree is completely saved, you are returned to the main Menu Builder menu. You can exit from here to your worksheet's Ready mode.

The option to save a set of menus as an alternate menu tree refers to Quattro's ability to switch between two sets of menus without exiting the program. Usually used to switch from the regular Quattro menus to 1-2-3 menus, this feature requires that one menu tree be a normal .RSC file and that the other be an alternative file with the .ALT extension, created by the Alternate Menu Tree option.

Using the New Menu

Unfortunately, you cannot use your new menu tree the moment you return to Ready mode. First you must update the .DEF file to let Quattro know which menus you would like loaded on startup. Use the /Default Startup Menu Tree command. To pick a menu tree, select Main Menus and choose from the list of .RSC files that will be displayed. If you are going to enter a simplified menu tree, you may want to maintain a full menu set, such as QUATTRO.ALT, as the Alternate Menus choices. This will allow you to use the Switch Menus option to gain quick access to the full set of commands if you need to perform system maintenance.

Having made your menu choices, select Update from the Menu Tree menu and quit Quattro. When you reload Quattro the specified main menu will be displayed when you press the / key.

Remember that to use the feature that lets you have two menu trees loaded into memory at the same time and to switch between them, you will need to leave the /Default Startup Menu Tree command somewhere in the menu tree. The menu tree you plan to use most of the time during a session is the Normal Menu Tree selection, whereas an alternative set of menus that you switch to during a session is the Alternate Menu Tree selection and is a compressed set of information about the menus stored in a file with the .ALT extension.

Since loading an alternate menu tree uses up 16K of memory you may not want to use an alternate menu tree unless it is really necessary.

If the menu tree you designed does not include the Default menu options somewhere within it, you will find it difficult to change the menu tree choice back to the default of QUATTRO.RSC. To prevent this dilemma, create a backup copy of your current .DEF file before recording the new menu as the default. Use the /File OS command to temporarily exit to DOS, and copy the current default file (normally QUATTRO.DEF) to another filename, such as BACKUP.DEF. Return to Quattro and use the /Default Startup Menu Tree command to make the new menu the one you want.

Having preserved the previous version of the .DEF file, you can safely record the new menu as the regular one with the Update option. For the change to be effective, you must exit from Quattro and reload the program. The new menu will now be active.

To return to the old menu, you can use the /Default Startup Menu Tree command and specify the previous .RSC file as the Main Menus selection. As an alternative, you can copy the BACKUP.DEF back to QUATTRO.DEF. Yet another option is to specify the old .DEF file from the DOS command line when you start Quattro, as in Q\DBACKUP.DEF.

PRINT COMMANDS

Quattro provides a wide range of options for printing from the spreadsheet. You can choose which cells to print and what size of paper to print on.

/Print Block

The /Print Block command specifies the area of the spreadsheet that you want to be sent to the printer. You should exclude any cells that are in heading areas. You can exclude columns within the block by using the /Column Hide command.

This command requires you to identify the cells in question. Only one block will be retained as part of the worksheet settings. Printing multiple blocks should be done by naming the blocks.

/Print Left Heading

The /Print Left Heading command selects a column or connected columns of labels to be repeated on successive pages of a long report. This allows you to give a title to the data being printed.

The /Print Left Heading command's only requirement is that you indicate the columns to be used. Include only the cells that are required.

Tip Areas included in a heading should be excluded from the print block.

/Print Top Heading

The /Print Top Heading command selects a row or connected rows of labels to be repeated on successive pages of a long report. This lets you give a title to the data being printed.

The /Print Top Heading command's only requirement is that you indicate the rows to be used.

/Print Destination

The /Print Destination command allows you to divert output from the printer to a file, usually so that the data can be read by another program (such as a word processor).

To use this command you must choose between Printer and File. If you choose File, you must give a file name. The default extension is .PRN. The default storage area is the same as that used for worksheets.

/Print Page Layout

The /Print Page Layout command is the command in which you specify how the printed output is to be arranged on the page.

This command requires you to choose which settings you want to adjust. The Header option lets you enter text to be repeated at the top of every page. The Footer option lets you enter text to be repeated at the bottom of every page. The Break Pages option lets you suppress the normal action of dividing the output between pages. The Margins and Length option lets you set page length, top and bottom margins (measured in lines), and left and right margins (measured in characters). The Create Break option lets you place a page-break code in the spreadsheet, forcing the output to be split onto another page at that line. The Setup String option is used to enter codes that control the type of print used by your printer. To record any of these settings for future use, use the Update option.

/Print Format

The /Print Format command is used to choose between a normal printing of the spreadsheet (As Displayed) and a listing of each the contents and coordinates of each occupied cell (Cell-Formulas).

This command requires you to choose between the As Displayed and Cell-Formulas options.

/Print Adjust Printer

The /Print Adjust Printer command is used to send instructions directly to the printer.

To use this command, you must have your printer turned on and loaded with paper. You can then select Skip Line to advance the paper one line in the printer. Choosing Form Feed will advance the paper a whole sheet. If you select Align, Quattro will know that the current position of the paper is correct to begin printing. Use Align before each print job to ensure correct positioning of output on paper.

/Print Reset

The /Print Reset command is used to reset printer settings.

This command requires you to choose between the Reset options of All, Print Block, Borders, or Layout.

/Print Go

The /Print Go command initiates the printing process.

To use this command, you must have your printer turned on and loaded with paper. You can stop printing by pressing CTRL-BREAK (CTRL-SCROLL LOCK).

PROTECTION COMMANDS

Quattro has several commands that help you protect the contents of spreadsheet cells. This provides a means of securing data and preserving model integrity.

/Default Protection Enable

The /Default Protection Enable command turns on global protection to prevent any cell of the spreadsheet from being changed. The exception is cells specifically unprotected with the /Block Advanced Unprotect command.

The /Default Protection Enable command simply requires you to select it. Worksheets saved with protection enabled will be protected when retrieved.

/Default Protection Disable

The /Default Protection Disable command turns off the global protection of the worksheet.

This command's only requirement is that you must select it.

QUIT COMMANDS

The Quattro menu has a Quit option that ends the current Quattro session and returns you to DOS or to any further commands in the batch file that was used to load Quattro. If you have not saved the latest changes to your current worksheet, you will be prompted to answer Yes or No before the Quit command completes.

There are Quit options on many of Quattro's submenus. These take you back to Ready mode from within a menu.Since there are so many Quit options, they are not all described in separate command sections.

RECALCULATION COMMANDS

Quattro uses "intelligent recalculation" to speed spreadsheet operations. You can control several aspects of the recalculation process.

/Default Recalculation Mode

The /Default Recalculation Mode command changes the way in which Quattro recalculates the worksheet when a new entry is made.

This command requires you to choose between Automatic (which means that every change that affects other cells is immediately reflected in an update of those cells); and Manual (which means that changes that affect other cells are not reflected until the F9 key is used to force a recalculation of the entire spreadsheet).

Tips Use Manual mode for faster data entry in large worksheets. Watch for the "CALC" message at the bottom of the screen; this indicates that unregistered changes have been made. Always press F9 before printing to ensure correct output. Use /Block Copy to copy cells on top of themselves in order to recalculate part of a worksheet.

► /Default Recalculation Order

The /Default Recalculation Order command changes the order in which Quattro calculates cells.

To use this command, choose between Natural, the default setting and safest choice, and either Rowwise or Columnwise, which are used for special formulas or for compatibility with older spreadsheet designs.

► /Default Recalculation Iteration

The /Default Recalculation Iteration command is used to set the number of times Quattro will review cells when calculating.

This command requires you to set at least two iterations with Recalc modes other than Natural unless you have a specific formula that requires otherwise.

/Default Recalculation Circular Cell

The /Default Recalculation Circular Cell option is not a command; it is a place to look for the address of cells causing circular references in a spreadsheet (indicated by the message "CIRC" at the bottom of the screen).

This option requires no action, but you should check the source of unexpected circular references and change them.

/Default Recalculation Quit

The /Default Recalculation Quit command offers a quick way out of the menu and back to Ready mode.

This command's only requirement is that you select it.

REGRESSION COMMANDS

Quattro has a built-in set of commands that perform regression analysis on spreadsheet data. The regression commands, found in the Advanced section of the main menu, produce a table of results.

The /Advanced Regression command is a means of performing regression analysis on numerical data that you have entered into your spreadsheet. The result of using the regression commands is a table showing the following elements: constant, standard error of Y estimate, R squared, number of observations, degrees of freedom, X coefficient(s), and standard error of coefficient.

The /Advanced Regression command requires you to define the block of cells containing the independent and dependent variables, the area of cells to use for the output table, and a Y intercept if you wish to specify one rather than have it computed. You then use the Go option on the /Advanced Regression menu to initiate the analysis. When performing analysis of several different groups of data in the same spreadsheet, you can change the /Advanced Regression settings with the Reset option.

STARTUP COMMANDS

Several program settings are grouped under Startup on the Default menu. These affect the way in which Quattro operates.

Autoload File

The autoload file is a specially named worksheet file that Quattro looks for every time the program is loaded. The worksheet bearing this name is automatically loaded as soon as the program is loaded. Initially, this name is set to QUATTRO.WKQ, but you can change it (to AUTO123.WK1, for example). This provides a certain amount of automation in running Quattro. When you select the Autoload File option, you type in your choice and press ENTER.

Startup Macro

Any worksheet that contains a macro that has the startup macro's name will run that macro as soon as the spreadsheet is loaded. Usually, this name is \0, but you can change it (for example, to FIRST). This provides a certain amount of automation in running a macro. When you select the Startup Macro option, you type in your choice and press ENTER.

Extension

Normal Quattro spreadsheet files have the extension .WKQ. You can have files saved in other formats by specifying a different extension; for example, you can use .WK1 so that the file can be read by 1-2-3 users or .WKZ so that it will be compressed by SQZ!. Making one of these or the other extensions the default extension automates the file conversion or compression feature. When you select the Extension option, you type in your choice and press ENTER.

Beep

Quattro beeps when you press an invalid key—for example, when you press HOME and then up arrow. If you find this annoying, you can turn off the beep by selecting the Beep option and then selecting No.

Help Access Method

When you press F1 for help, Quattro looks for the QUATTRO.HLP file. If you are using a floppy disk system, you may need to insert the appropriate disk for Quattro to find this file. Hard disk users will always have this file available in the resource directory; they can speed up Help key response by selecting Help Access Method and then choosing Instant. The alternative is the Removable option; floppy disk users should select this. In fact, you cannot select Instant unless you have a hard disk.

Default Add-Ins

The additional programs that work with Quattro, such as Menu Builder and Transcript, are called *add-ins.*

You can have as many as eight of them to be loaded automatically when the Quattro program loads. In the case of Transcript, this ensures constant recording of all keystrokes. In the case of Menu Builder, this means that the program is immediately available with the /Macro Run command.

When you select Default Add-Ins, you can enter up to eight names by highlighting the numbers 1 through 8 in turn and pressing ENTER for a list of add-in programs (extension .QAI) in the resource directory. You can also use Reset to change the selection and Update to record the selection into the .DEF file. You will have to end the current session and reload Quattro for this change to be effective.

Menu Tree

Quattro's menu choices, their actions and their descriptions are stored in a file with the extension .RSC. The usual menu system, or tree, is stored in QUATTRO.RSC. Another menu tree, with choices arranged as they are in 1-2-3, is stored in 123.RSC. You can make either of these menu trees (or others that you design yourself with Menu Builder), the default system of menus.

When you select Menu Tree, you have several options. You can specify your choice for the main menus, the ones that are normally displayed by the / key and that have the .RSC extension. You can also specify alternative menus to be switched to during a Quattro session. An alternate menu has the extension .ALT and is a compressed version of a regular menu tree created by Menu Builder. The Reset Alternate option lets you clear the choice for the Alternate Menus optionn.

The Switch Menus option lets you activate either the Main Menus choice or the Alternate Menus choice. The Update option lets you record your choices in the .DEF file. You will have to end the current session and reload Quattro for this change to be effective.

Compatibility Options

To allow Quattro to conform to the expectations of users familiar with other programs, there are a number of options that can be changed to provide compatibility. When you select Compatibility Options, you find several items, most of which are set to Yes or No.

Setting the Keep Wide option to Yes means that all menus, except for the file and function lists, will automatically be shown in their wide format. Setting this option to No keeps them narrower. You can always use the gray plus and minus keys to expand and contract menus.

Setting Remember to Yes means that Quattro will highlight the last item you picked from a menu when you return to that menu. Otherwise, Quattro highlights the first item on the menu. Borland Style, under the Confirm Options section, refers to the prompts you get to remind you that you are about to lose data. Setting these prompts to No will match the 1-2-3 style of confirmation. Setting the During Macros option to No will make the macros compatible with 1-2-3.

Setting the Macro Recording option to Logical records your keystrokes in menu equivalents. Setting it to Keystroke records keystrokes as actual keys pressed. There is an Update option on the Compatibility Options menu allows you to record your choices in the .DEF file.

TRANSCRIPT COMMANDS

You activate the Transcript add-in by using /Macro Load and specifying TRANS.QAI as the add-in to be loaded. All of your work will then be recorded to a log file on disk. You can access this record by using the /Macro Run command and specifying Transcript. The log of keystrokes is presented, complete with date and time information. You can acccss the Transcript menu at this time by pressing the / key. The menu allows you to undo the last command, which is helpful when you have erased material accidentally. You can restore the spreadsheet to the current point. You can play back a block of commands and copy keystrokes from the log to the spreadsheet for use in macros. Use Begin Block and End Block to mark the section of the log you want to play back or copy.

You can see the current setting of the Transcript log size in the Max Hist Length option. This is normally 2,000 bytes. The name of this log file on disk is QUATTRO.LOG. When the log reaches the size limit, it is renamed QUATTROBAQ.LOG and a new QUATTRO.LOG is started. You can set the history length from 1 to 25,000 bytes.

When you want to play back from the log, you can do so one keystroke at a time, by using the Single step command. You can interrupt playback with the CTRL-BREAK (SCROLL LOCK) key. If you find that storing your keystrokes with Transcript slows down your work you can turn off the Failure Protection feature. This will prevent each keystroke from being written to disk as you type it. Instead, Transcript will store the keys in a buffer and only record periodically. This improves speed, but may mean that disaster recovery is not as complete.

TRANSLATE AND COMPRESS COMMANDS

When you use the /File Save or /File Xtract commands, Quattro will store your spreadsheet data in any one of a dozen different file formats (depending upon the filename extension that you assign when saving the file). The .WKQ extension signifies a standard Quattro file. A file with the .WKZ extension is a compressed Quattro file that is reduced in size by the SQZ! option (which uses the settings you specify with the /File !SQZ! command). The .WKS extension signifies a 1-2-3 Release 1A file (the .WK$ extension indicates a SQZ! compressed version of the same format). A file with .WK1 as an extension is a 1-2-3 Release 2 file (the .WK! extension indicates a compressed version of the same format). A Symphony file has the .WRK extension and a Reflex database file has the .RXD extension. The .DBF extension signifies a dBASEIII database file and the .DB2 extension indicates a dBASE II database file (convert to .DBF after saving to disk). The .DB extension is used for a Paradox database file.

All database files store Quattro spreadsheets as though they are laid out as a Quattro database (consecutive rows of records in contiguous columns headed by field names). Use /File Extract rather than /File Save when first creating a non-Quattro database file. Store values instead of formulas. You will be prompted to review the field names and types before completing the extract or save.

Quattro will read data from Reflex, dBASE, and Paradox in the form of a row-and-column database. Simply specify the full name if the database file when using the /File Retrieve command. Note that Quattro will resave to the same filename by default and so you will need to change the extension to convert the data to a Quattro file. Use the space bar at the file name prompt to place the filename line in edit mode. Then backspace over the extension you want to change. Alternatively press ESCAPE at the filename prompt and type in a completely new name.

UPDATE COMMANDS

When you are using /Default commands, several of the menus you will see contain the Update option. When you select this option, the current default settings are recorded in a configuration file. The usual name for this file is QUATTRO.DEF. Use the Update command to save settings from one session to another. If you do not use this command after making changes to program settings in the Default menu, the changes will be lost and the settings will revert to the way they were before you made the changes.

The role of the .DEF file is important when you are customizing Quattro. When you load Quattro by means of the Q command and ENTER at the DOS prompt, Quattro looks for a file called QUATTRO.DEF from which to load default settings. If it does not find this file, the program runs with the original default settings. If you load without a QUATTRO.DEF file in place and then save changes to the defaults with the /Default Update command, a file called QUATTRO.DEF will be created. You can use copies of this file as the basis for multiple customized versions of Quattro. If you copy QUATTRO.DEF to MYQ.DEF and then load Quattro with the command Q/DMYQ.DEF, Quattro will load settings from the MYQ.DEF file. Your changes to the defaults will be recorded into MYQ.DEF when you use the Update command.

WHAT-IF COMMANDS

These commands are used to perform sensitivity analyses on your data.

/Advanced What-if 1 Variable

The /Advanced What-if 1 Variable command allows you to substitute various values for a single spreadsheet variable and produce a table of the results (often called a *one-way* data table). For example, you may want to determine the total revenue, gross profit, and net profit from a five-year projection based on a variety of initial sales figures. This table is a collection of the results of calculations—it is not dynamic, and so it will not be updated automatically once it is created.

The /Advanced What-if 1 Variable command requires a table consisting of a column of values that will be input into the formulas, such as the starting sales figures in a projection; and a row consisting of the formulas, beginning on the row above the top of the input column and one column to the right. The formulas can reference existing cells containing formulas, such as the total revenue, gross profit, and net profit, or the formulas can be new ones. The row of formulas is the top of the table, and the column of values is the left edge.

When you select 1 Variable from the What-if menu, you are prompted for the block of cells to use as the data table. This begins with the cell above the first input value and to the left of the first formula and extends to the cell that is in the last row of the input values and the column of the last formula. When you enter this block, you are prompted for an input cell. This is the cell in the model into which you want Quattro to place the input values, one after another; for example, the cell that has the initial sales figure of a projection. When you enter this cell, Quattro will run the input values through the input cell and will list, adjacent to their respective input values, the resulting values of each of the formulas in the top row of the table.

/Advanced What-if 2 Variables

The /Advanced What-if 2 Variables command allows you to substitute various values into two different variable cells in a spreadsheet and to produce a table of the results (often called a *two-way* data table). For example, you may want to determine the net profit from a five-year projection based on a variety of initial revenue and expense figures. This table is a collection of the results of calculations; it is not dynamic, so it will not be updated automatically once it is created.

The /Advanced What-if 2 Variables command requires a table consisting of a column of values that will be input into one cell of the model, such as the starting revenue figure in a projection; and a row of values that will be input into another variable, such as starting expenses. This row is placed one row above the top of the input column and one column to the right.

When you select 2 Variable from the What-if menu, you are prompted for the block of cells to use as the data table. This begins with the cell above the first value in the input column and to the left of the first value in the input row, and extends to the cell that is in the last row of the input values and the column of the row value. When you enter this block, you are prompted for the first input cell. This is the cell in the model into which you want Quattro to place the input values from the column. When you enter this cell, you are prompted for the second input cell, the one into which the values from the row will be placed. When you enter this cell, Quattro will run the input values through the input cells and will list, adjacent to their respective input values, the resulting values in the model.

/Advanced What-If Reset

The /Advanced What-if Reset command lets you change all of the What-if settings. Since these settings are usually retained in order to facilitate the repetition of the last table command, you must either use Reset when moving on to a different set of parameters or change each one individually as you execute the 1 Variable or 2 Variable command.

The /Advanced What-if Reset command requires only that you select it. You are left at the What-if menu.

/Advanced What-if Quit

The /Advanced What-if Quit command returns you from the What-If menu to Ready mode. The ESCAPE key takes you from the What-if menu to the the Advanced menu.

This command requires only that you select it.

FORMULAS AND FUNCTIONS

The heart of Quattro's power to manipulate information is its ability to create formulas. Quattro formulas combine values (such as a number or a cell containing a number) with operators and built-in functions, which are preceded by the @ sign.

The plus sign (+) is used in front of cell names and block names that begin formulas so that Quattro can recognize them as values and not labels. Quattro formulas are algebraic in format. Thus, you can use formulas within a formula, separated or delimited by pairs of parentheses, as in the following:

```
E13 = ((E6*E7)+(E9*E10))*2
```

This means that in E13, Quattro should multiply E6 by E7, add that to the product of E9 multiplied by E10, and then double the answer.

Formulas that contain several elements are common, as when you request Quattro to make decisions about the data to be calculated. For example, the formula

```
B6 = @IF(0.25*B5<30000,0.25*B5,30000)
```

This formula tells Quattro that the amount in B6 should be 25% of the amount in B5, unless that figure is more than 30,000, in which case B6 should be 30,000.

Note that formulas do not have spaces in them when entered into Quattro. This is a general rule in all Quattro formulas. You will also notice that Quattro capitalizes cell references, block names, and function names when you enter a formula. It does not matter if you enter these as upper- or lowercase; Quattro will store and display them as uppercase. Block names used in formulas are shown as cell coordinates when editing.

Values

The values in a Quattro formula can be the coordinates of cells containing values, a block of cells containing values (either stated as coordinates, or described by block names), functions (like @RAND), or constants (a *constant* is a number, date, or piece of text that you enter directly, such as the 1 in 1+B3).

Operators

The operators used in Quattro formulas are arithmetic operators. These include the basic add, subtract, multiply, and divide operators:

```
+  -  *  /
```

Another operator, the exponent operator (^), translates as "to the power of" when attached to a number.

The order of priority between different operators in the same formula is the natural mathematical order. Multiplication and division are done before addition and subtraction. If all of the operators are the same, as in 2*3*4 (=24), then the calculation is performed from left to right. You can affect the order of calculation by using parentheses, as in the following:

```
2*3+4=10
2*(3+4)=14
```

When you nest calculations within several parentheses, the innermost calculations are performed first. In the formula ((E6*E7)+(E9*E10))*2, the arrangement of parentheses means that both E6*E7 and E9*E10 will occur before the *2 part, which stands outside of the parentheses.

Entering Formulas

Formulas can be created in several different ways. You can look at the worksheet and decide which cells are involved, and then type their addresses into the formula. The more cautious spreadsheet user (and the less adept typist) might prefer the pointing method of entering formulas. This begins with the plus sign (or another appropriate value indicator), which places Quattro in Value mode. You then use the arrow keys to highlight the first cell you want in the formula. When you do this, Quattro types the cell address for you. You can then type the next math sign or value indicator and the cell selector will move back down to the cell in which you are building the formula. The basic sequence is math sign, point, math sign, point. You can point to each cell that needs to go into the formula and it is added on the edit line at the top of the screen as you build the formula. The completed formula is placed into the original cell with the ENTER key.

This method is very useful when you have several cells scattered throughout the spreadsheet and cannot remember where a particular number is. The pointing method can be used effectively with formulas that involve functions.

Functions and Blocking

Some formulas and functions use blocks of cells. These can be typed in directly by entering the diagonal coordinates of the block as you create the formula. As an alternative, you can use the pointing method to block out the cells to be included, anchoring the upper-left corner by pressing the period key, and then using the down and right arrows to complete highlighting of the block.

After Entering a Formula

When you have entered a formula, the result of the formula—not the formula itself—is displayed in the cell. However, the cell identifier shows the formula—not the value—whenever you highlight a cell that contains a formula. You may not want the value generated by the formula to be dynamic and change when the worksheet is recalculated. To fix a value, you can convert the formula to the value it produces. This can be done in two ways. If you press F2 while you are highlighting the cell that contains the formula, the formula will be placed on the edit line at the top of the screen. If you press the Calc key (F9), the formula will be turned into its result, which can then be placed into the cell with the ENTER key. As an alternative, you can use the /Block Advanced Values command to convert a block of cells from formulas to values.

Named Blocks

The naming of blocks is useful for developing formulas, because block names can be used instead of cell coordinates. Even attaching a name to a single cell is productive. It is often easier to type LENGTH*WIDTH than to type H5*H6. You do not need to check where these elements are and do not need to take time pointing them out. Furthermore, if you type H555*H6 by mistake, Quattro will not tell you that this is an error. On the other hand, if you try to enter an invalid block name, Quattro will beep and place you in Edit mode so that you can correct the mistake.

Many people find that block names are easier to use than cell coordinates for groups of cells. It is much easier to type @SUM(COUNTY) than it is to type @SUM(G16.G18). The benefits of block names rapidly increase as you create more formulas; for example, @SUM(COUNTY,STATE) is a lot easier to type than @SUM(G16..G18,H16..H18), particularly when you can press the Choices key (F3) to display a list of block names from which to choose.

Editing Formulas

If there is a mistake in a formula that you are creating, such as a misspelled block or function name, an invalid cell reference, or an unrecognized symbol, Quattro will not accept the formula when you press ENTER. Instead, it will beep, change to Edit mode, and attempt to position the edit cursor near the error you have made. Formulas are always edited on the edit line and are placed there either by Quattro when it rejects a formula or by you when you need to change a previously entered formula. To begin editing a formula, you highlight the cell and press F2 to enter Edit mode. The formula will be displayed on the edit line for editing.

Formula Errors

If you spell a formula correctly but use improper elements within it, Quattro displays the error message "Syntax Error". Check the formula to find the error. Quattro attempts to put the cursor near the error, so look there first. You may have neglected to close a pair of parentheses or quotation marks, or you may have omitted the @ sign before a function name. A common mistake is placing spaces between the elements of a formula. Although documentation occasionally seems to show them, spaces generally are not allowed in formulas.

Named blocks must be spelled correctly. The Choices key (F3) lets you select from a list of block names when you are writing formulas.

You may succeed in entering a formula only to see "CIRC" in the status line. This means that the formula refers to itself, which will not work. You cannot, for example, ask Quattro to multiply the current cell by 2 and put the answer in the current cell. This kind of problem is solved by retyping the formula. (Check the /Default Recalculation menu for the location of the circular reference cell.)

A similar problem is to refer to an as-yet-unnamed block in your formula. When this happens, you must stop typing the formula and name the block. You can avoid this problem by defining a named block as soon as you create it and by using the Choices key to select block names.

One trick to save the typing you have already done on a rejected formula is to press HOME when Quattro places you in Edit mode. Then type an apostrophe. This allows you to enter the formula as a label and then review it. When you edit the formula and are ready to reenter it as a value, simply press HOME and then DELETE to remove the apostrophe before you press ENTER.

FUNCTIONS—THE BUILT-IN FORMULAS

Quattro provides you with the basic building blocks of complex formulas in the form of *functions*. These built-in formulas are specially coded commands that facilitate typical calculations and save you from entering lengthy instructions. Some functions simply generate values by themselves. For example, @PI gives you the value of pi. However, most functions require additional information in the form of an *argument*. For example, the principal, interest, and term required by the @PMT function are called the arguments for @PMT. Some functions require just one argument (such as @SUM, which just needs to know what block of cells you want to sum), while others (such as @PMT) require several arguments.

Numeric functions can reference a mixture of cell coordinates and block names, as in @PMT(E1, INTEREST, TERM). Functions are often combined with operators and values in formulas, just like any other formula element.

Function Syntax

In addition to the distinction between numeric and string functions, which closely follows that between values and labels, functions can be grouped by the type of work they apply to: financial, date, logical, and so on. However, all Quattro functions are always entered in the same basic format, using a standard arrangement of parts known as the *syntax* for functions:

- Functions begin with a leading @ sign.
- The @ sign is followed by the name of the function, typed in uppercase, lowercase, or a combination, and spelled accurately.
- Arguments, when required, are enclosed in parentheses and follow the function name.
- When using multiple arguments, the arguments be separated by commas and the arguments must be in proper order.
- No spaces are allowed between the @ sign and the function name.

A function with its arguments (if any) is referred to as a *function statement*. If you try to enter a function statement that contains an error (for example, an incorrectly spelled function name), Quattro will beep and place the entry on the edit line. It will also attempt to place the edit-line cursor in the area of the mistake. This can be very helpful if, for example, you have omitted a comma between arguments or left a pair of parentheses unclosed.

The Choices Key

One way to prevent such errors as misspelled function names is to use the Function Choices key (ALT-F3). Pressing this key when you are either in Ready mode or Edit mode displays a list of functions. You can then browse through this list with the arrow keys, moving a page at a time with PGUP and PGDN. When you see the function that you need, you can highlight it and press ENTER to place the function on the edit line. If you are not sure of the appropriate function, you can press the plus key on the numeric pad, which will expand the menu to show the arguments each function requires. You can pull function names onto the edit line from both the wide and narrow versions of the Choices menu.

@Functions Listed By Category

Mathematical Functions

@ABS(number)
@ACOS(number)
@ASIN(number)
@ATAN(number)
@ATAN2(number1/number2)
@COS(number)
@DEGREES(radians)
@EXP(number)
@INT(number)
@LN(number)
@LOG(number)
@MOD(number,divisor)
@PI
@RADIANS(degrees)
@RAND
@ROUND(number,decimal places)
@SIN(number)
@SQRT(number)
@TAN(number)

Aggregation and Counting Functions

@AVG(list)
@COUNT(list)
@MAX(list)

@MIN(list)
@STD(list)
@SUM(list)
@VAR(list)

String Functions

@CHAR(number)
@CLEAN(string)
@CODE(string)
@EXACT(string1,string2)
@FIND(search string,target string,start location)
@HEXTONUM(string)
@LEFT(string,number of characters)
@LENGTH(string)
@LOWER(string)
@MID(string,start number,number of
characters)
@N(Block)
@NUMTOHE(number)
@PROPER(string)
@REPEAT(string,number of times to repeat)
@REPLACE(string to replace,start location,number
of characters,newstring)
@RIGHT(string,number of characters)
@S(Block)
@STRING(number,decimal places)
@TRIM(string)
@UPPER(string)

@VALUE(string)

Miscellaneous Functions

@@(cell address)
@CELL(attribute,block)
@CELLINDEX(attribute,block,col offset,row offset)
@CELLPOINTER(attribute)
@COLS(block)
@CURVALUE(generalization,specification)
@ERR
@ISERR(value)
@ISNA(value)
@ISNUMBER(value)
@ISSTRING(string)
@MEMAVAIL
@MEMEMSAVAIL
@NA
@ROWS(block)

Logical Functions

@CHOOSE(number,list)
@FALSE
@HLOOKUP(number to look up,table,row number in table)
@IF(condition,action if true,action if false)
@INDEX(table location,column number,row number)

@FILEEXISTS(filename)
@TRUE
@VLOOKUP(number to look up,table,column number in table)

Financial Functions

@CTERM(interest,future value,present value)
@DDB(cost,salvage value,life of property,period)
@FV(payment,interest,term)
@IRR(guess,list of values)
@NPV(interest,list of cash flows)
@PMT(principle,interest,term)
@PV(principle,interest,term)
@RATE(future value,present value,term)
@SLN(cost,salvage value,life of property)
@SYD(cost,salvage value,life of property, period)
@TERM(payment,interest,future value)

Date and Time Functions

@DATE(year,month,day)
@DATEVALUE(datestring)
@DAY(datenumber)
@HOUR(timenumber)
@MINUTE(timenumber)
@MONTH(datenumber)
@NOW

@SECOND(timenumber)
@TIME(hour,minute,second)
@TIMEVALUE(timestring)
@TODAY
@YEAR(datenumber)

Database Aggregation Functions

@DAVG(input block,column,criteria)
@DCOUNT(input block,column,criteria)
@DMAX(input block,column,criteria)
@DMIN(input block,column,criteria)
@DSTD(input,block,column,criteria)
@DSUM(input block,column,criteria)
@DVAR(input block,column,criteria)

MACROS

A *macro* consists of instructions stored in a series of spreadsheet cells. The instructions are entered as labels, using either the exact keys you press (as in / FR for the / File Retrieve command) or as command equivalents (as in {/ File Retrieve}). The menu equivalents are used by Quattro when it records your commands, both in the ALT-F8 (or ALT-minus) Record mode and in the Transcript Log. Macro instructions can be executed by the /Macro Execute command, either by pointing at the first cell in the series or by referring to it by name with the F3 key.You can create 26 instant macros, named \ A through \ Z, that are activated by the ALT key and the letter. You are allowed any number of macros named with block names. These are activated by pressing F8 and then entering the name or choosing it from the list that is displayed.

Macro Recording

You can write macros directly into cells. Use the SHIFT-F3 key to display a list of macro commands and menu equivalents that can be used in macros. You can also record any action you want to include in a macro by using the ALT-F8 key combination (or ALT-minus key) to begin recording and the same key to end recording. Recorded actions are placed in the named cells you indicate. You can use an instant macro name (\A-\Z) or any other valid block name. Use the /Default Startup Compatibility Macro Recording Keystroke command to tell Quattro to record actual keystrokes. Use the /Default Startup Compatibility Macro Recording Logical command to record in menu equivalents.

Startup Macro

You can have Quattro activate a macro as soon as the file in which it is stored is retrieved. This Startup macro is usually called \0, but you can use a different name (such as FIRST) as long as you record your name with the /Default Startup and the /Default Update commands. Use of the Startup macro goes hand in hand with the Autoload file, a worksheet file that is retrieved from disk as soon as Quattro is loaded. The file that Quattro looks for when it is loaded is normally called QUATTRO.WKQ, but you can change it to another name such as FIRST.WKQ by using the /Default Startup menu. If you create a Startup macro in a worksheet named as the Autoload file, you can initiate any series of events that macros can control.

Command-Line Macros

If you want to load Quattro and then a particular spreadsheet, you can do so without using the Autoload file feature. Simply type the name of the file after the name of the program when you are loading from the DOS prompt or command line. For example, if you type **Q PRICING** when you have turned on your PC and are at the DOS prompt ready to load Quattro, the program will load and immediately retrieve the worksheet called PRICING.WKQ.

You can name a macro on the command line as well. If you have a macro in the PRICING worksheet called QUOTE you could type **Q PRICING QUOTE** at the DOS prompt, press ENTER, and have the program load itself, the worksheet called PRICING.WKQ, and the macro called QUOTE.

Macro Executing Key (F8)

The F8 key displays an alphaetical list of macros. To execute one of them you highlight the macro name and press ENTER. This is an easy way to provide users with a menu of available macros. The names can be up to sixteen characters long and thus can be quite descriptive.

Macro Language

Quattro allows you to add logic to macros, which allows you to create macros that evaluate conditions and choose between different courses of action based on the parameters you specify. This is done by means of *Macro commands*, a set of commands that are not keystroke or menu equivalents, but programming statements.

MACRO COMMANDS

The following list of Macro commands is organized by type of command: screen, interactive, program flow, cell, and file I/O.

Screen

{PANELOFF}: disables updating of control panel
{PANELON}: enables updating of control panel
{WINDOWSOFF}: disables worksheet display update
{WINDOWSON}: enables worksheet display update
{INDICATE string}: controls mode indicator display

Interactive

{?}: pauses for user input
{GET location}: takes input from keyboard
{GETLABEL prompt,location}: prompts for user-entered label
{GETNUMBER prompt,location}: prompts for user-entered number
{LOOK location}: checks keyboard buffer for keystroke
{BEEP pitchnumber}: sounds beep
{MENUCALL location}: displays and transfers control to menu

{MENUBRANCH location}: displays and transfers control to menu

{WAIT date-timevalue}: pauses program for time period

Program Flow

{BRANCH location}: transfers program control

{FOR counter,start,stop,step,routine}: manages repeating subroutine

{FORBREAK}: interrupts {For} command

{IF condition}: controls program based on condition

{ONERROR branch,message}: traps program control if error occurs

{RETURN}: ends subroutine

{QUIT}: stops macro execution

{DEFINE location1:type1,...}: places parameter in cell

{DISPATCH location}: transfers program control

{BREAKON}: enables CTRL-BREAK

{BREAKOFF}: disables CTRL-BREAK

{STEPON}: enables DEBUG

{STEPOFF}: disables DEBUG

{;}: explanatory remarks

{ }: blank line

Cells

{BLANK location}: erases specified block
{CONTENTS destination,source,width,format}: enters string in cell
{LET location,value:type}: enters argument result in cell
{PUT block,column,row,value:type}: enters argument result in cell
{RECALC location,condition,iteration}: recalculates rows of worksheet
{RECALCCOL location,condition,iteration}: recalculates columns of worksheet

File I/O

{FILESIZE location}: returns measure of file size
{OPEN filename,mode}: opens files
{GETPOS location}: returns position of file pointer
{READ bytecount,location}: reads data from open file
{READLN location}: reads data from open file
{SETPOS file-position}: positions file pointer
{WRITE bytes,output-string}: writes string to file
{WRITELN output-string}: writes string to file with CR/LF
{CLOSE}: closes file

/x Equivalents

/xc: **{subroutine}**
/xl: **{GETLABEL}**
/xn: **{GETNUMBER}**
/xg: **{BRANCH}**
/xi: **{IF}**
/xm: **{MENUBRANCH}**
/xq: **{QUIT}**
/xr: **{RETURN}**

Debug

The Debug command (SHIFT-F8), provides you with single-step macro execution. To see the macro execute in single-step mode, you repeatedly press the space bar. While you are executing a macro in debug mode, you can press / to get the Macro Debugging menu. The Edit a Cell option allows you to edit the current cell of the macro, removing errors that you have noticed during the execution. If the macro appears to be fine during Debug playback, you can let it run to completion by pressing the ENTER key.

Breakpoints In addition to the single-step feature, you can also set *breakpoints* from the Macro Debugging Menu. These are blocks or cells of macro code at which the macro should pause during execution. Breakpoints area easier for testing sections of large macros than is inserting blank cells after the last line you want to execute. By pressing ENTER during Debug playback, you can run the macro to the next breakpoint. Up to four breakpoints can be set from the Macro Debugging Menu. If you want the breakpoint to be effective only on a repetition of the macro, you can set a pass count for the breakpoint. Use Reset from the Macro Debugging menu to clear the breakpoints.

Conditional If you want a macro to run until a particular condition is met, you can use the Conditional option on the Macro Debugging Menu to point to a cell in which you have entered a logical formula. An appropriate logical formula would be one that returns 1 for true or 0 for false. Thus, a cell containing the formula +A1>99 could be used to make the macro playback pause if it caused A1 to exceed 99.

Trace Cells If you are concerned with a macro's effect on particular cells of your spreadsheet, you can identify up to four trace cells, which will be monitored in the Trace Window during Debug mode. This is very helpful for running a large macro that affects diverse areas of the worksheet.

COMMONLY USED QUATTRO KEYS AND MACRO EQUIVALENTS

Key: Equivalent—Purpose

ENTER: **{cr}** or ~—to enter data into worksheet, select highlighted menu items, confirm block coordinates and other settings.

ESCAPE: **{esc}**—cancels changes on the Edit line, takes you out of menus, returns you to Ready mode, unlocks block coordinates

BACKSPACE: **{bs}**—removes characters to the left on the Edit line, unlocks block coordinates and returns beginning coordinate to current cell

DELETE: **{del}**—deletes cell contents, removes current character from Edit line

INS: **{ins}**—controls Overstrike mode when editing

SHIFT: none—to get upper half of any key, including capitals A-Z, symbols such as $, numbers on numeric pad

CAPS LOCK: none—makes A-Z type as capitals without shifting, does not affect any other keys

NUM LOCK: none—locks numeric pad into numbers, locks out cursor movement with those keys

CTRL: none—used with certain keys to execute commands, such as CTRL-BREAK which stops macro execution, CTRL- D which prepares cell for date entry, CTRL-ENTER which assigns Shortcuts

ALT: none—used with - to record keystrokes for macros, and with selected keys to execute macros

PRINT SCREEN: none—prints current screen, will not print graphs

@: none—precedes built-in formulas, the @Functions

/: none—in Ready mode activates Menu, in formulas for division

\ : used as Cell Fill command to repeat characters, also used in naming "instant" macros

+: none—both are used to begin formulas, perform addition, the one on the numeric pad expands menus {expand}

*: none—used for multiplication sign

-: none—used for subtraction, used with ALT to begin macro recording, the one on the numeric pad contracts menus **{contract}**

QUATTRO FUNCTION KEYS WITH MACRO EQUIVALENTS

F1: **{help}**—shows Help screen

ALT-F1: **{previous}**—shows last displayed Help Screen

F2: **{edit}**—allows editing of cells

F3: **{names}**—shows named blocks

SHIFT-F3: **{macros}**—displays list of macro commands

ALT-F3: **{functions}**—shows list of @Functions

F4: **{abs}**—shows cell references as absolute

F5: **{goto}**—moves cell selector to cell/named block

F6: **{window}**—moves cell selector to the other window

F7: **{query}**—repeats the last Query

ALT-F7 **{table}**—repeats the last What-if command

F8: **{macro}**—lists macros to execute

SHIFT-F8: **{debug}**—activates debug mode

ALT-F8: **{record}**—begins and ends macro recording

F9: **{calc}**—in Ready mode, recalculates all formulas when using manual calculation; in Edit mode converts formula to value.

F10: **{graph}**—displays the current Graph

QUATTRO EDIT MODE KEYS AND MACRO EQUIVALENTS

Key: Action—Equivalent

LEFT: **{left}** or **{L}**—moves cursor 1 character left

RIGHT: **{right}** or **{r}**—moves cursor 1 character right

HOME: **{home}**—moves cursor to first character

END: **{end}** moves cursor to the right of last character

TAB: **{big right}**—moves cursor 5 characters to the right

CTRL-RIGHT: **{big right}**—moves cursor 5 characters to the right

SHIFT-TAB: **{big left}**—moves cursor 5 characters to the left

CTRL-LEFT: **{big left}**—moves cursor 5 characters to the left

DEL: **{del}**—deletes character at cursor

INS: **{ins}**—toggles between insert and over-strike

BACKSPACE: **{bs}**—deletes character to left of cursor

ESCAPE: **{esc}**—cancels editing, returns to Ready mode

ENTER: **{cr}** or ~—enters contents

DOWN: **{down}** or **{d}**—enters contents

UP: **{up}** or **{u}**—enters contents

PAGE DOWN: **{pgdn}**—enters contents

PAGE UP: **{pgup}**—enters contents

QUATTRO FORMAT CHOICES

Format Name: Description of Format

Fixed: No commas in 1000s, user-defined decimal places: 2000.99, -2000.99

Scientific: Exponential notation, user-defined decimal places: 2.00E+03 -2.00E+03

Currency: Commas placed in 1,000s, negatives in parentheses, user-defined decimal places, uses default international currency symbol as a prefix or suffix: $2,000.99 ($2,000.99)

, (Financial): Commas placed in 1,000s, negatives in parentheses, user-defined decimal places: 2,000.99 (2,000.99)

General: Varies decimal places, uses exponential notation for large numbers

+/-: Represents positive numbers as plus signs (+), negatives as minus signs (-) for simple bar charts.

Percent: Divides contents by 100, uses % sign as suffix

Date: Various options, includes formats for Time values

Text (Show Formulas): Displays formulas in cells, rather than their values

Hidden: Hides cell contents from view, shows contents only on the descriptor line

FORMAT IDENTIFIERS

Code: Format
F0-F15: Financial (0-15 decimal places)
S0-S15: Scientific (0-15 decimal places)
C0-C15: Currency (0-15 decimal places)
,0-,15: Comma/Financial (0-15 decimal places)
G: General (variable decimal places)
P1-P15: Percentage (0-15 decimal places)
D1-D5: Date formats
D6-D9: Time formats

FILE LIST KEYS USED TO NAVIGATE A LIST OF FILES

Key: Action

DOWN: Down one file
TAB: Down one file
RIGHT: Down one file
UP: Up one file
SHIFT-TAB: Up one file
LEFT: Up one file
PAGE DOWN: One screen full down
PAGE UP: One screen full up
HOME: Top of the list
END: Bottom of the list